CIMA REVISION CARDS

Management Accounting Business Strategy

Neil Botten

Strategic Level Paper P6

ELSEVIER

AMSTERDAM • BOSTON • HEIDELBERG • LONDON • NEW YORK • OXFORD
PARIS • SAN DIEGO • SAN FRANCISCO • SINGAPORE • SYDNEY • TOKYO

Elsevier Butterworth-Heinemann
Linacre House, Jordan Hill, Oxford OX2 8DP
30, Corporate Drive, Burlington, MA 01803

First Published 2006

British Library Cataloguing in Publication Data
A catalogue record for this book is available from the British Library

Library of Congress Cataloging in Publication Data
A catalogue record for this book is available from the Library of Congress

ISBN 10: 0 7506 8119 5
ISBN 13: 978 0 7506 8119 3

For information on all Elsevier Butterworth-Heinemann publications visit our website at http://books.elsevier.com

Welcome to CIMA's Official Revision Cards. These cards have been designed to:

- Save you time by summarising the syllabus in a concise form
- Jog your memory through the use of diagrams and bullet points
- Follow the structure of the CIMA Official Learning Systems
- Refer to relevant questions found within the Preparing for the Examination section of the Learning System
- Provide you with plenty of exam tips and hints

Ensure exam success by revising with the only revision cards endorsed by CIMA.

TABLE OF CONTENTS

1. Setting the goals of the organisation 1
2. Appraising the environment 11
3. Position appraisal and analysis 27
4. Strategic aspects of marketing 47
5. Strategic implications of IT 71
6. Strategic options and their evaluation 89
7. Organisational impacts of business strategy 111
8. Implementing and controlling plans 123

Setting the Goals of the Organisation

Key learning system questions

1.1 Mission statements
1.2 Not-for-profit objectives
10 Identify relevant stakeholders
15 Identify relevant stakeholders

Topics

- Identity of stakeholders
- Corporate social responsibility
- Setting strategic objectives
- Critical success factors
- Objectives for shareholders
- Objectives for not-for-profit organisations
- Competing objectives

Identity of stakeholders

Stakeholders

Groups or individuals having a legitimate interest in the activities of an organisation

Stakeholders

⇨ Stakeholder groups, are relatively simple for commercial organisations
⇨ But are more numerous and complex for not-for-profits
⇨ Have different sources of power: expertise, access to resources, access to information, physical strength, charisma and network power
⇨ Have different claims on the organisation: economic, legal, ethical and discretionary

⇨ Can be mapped using Mendelow's matrix which plots stakeholder power against stakeholder interest
⇨ Different groups may have conflicting objectives
⇨ Firms must manage stakeholder expectations

Regarding stakeholders

Make sure you can identify different stakeholder groups in any question you have to deal with. Make sure you can gain an impression of their source of power and their likely interests. You should be in a position to advise the decision makers what steps they should take to manage stakeholders expectations. With most organisations there will be at least two groups with conflicting objectives

Corporate social responsibility

Corporate social responsibility

'The continuing commitment of business to behave ethically and contribute to economic development whilst improving the quality of life of the workforce and their families as well as of the local community and society at large'

Corporate social responsibility

⇨ How companies manage their business processes ought to have an overall positive effect on society

⇨ Not to be confused with business ethics which is about 'good behaviour' and is one element of CSR

⇨ Will become more important as globalisation increases since the power of the nation state will decline

Regarding CSR

You should be able to recognise situations where the company is not acting in an appropriate way and be able to make recommendations to decision makers suggesting how they can improve their performance in this respect

Strategic objectives are

⇨ Different to mission statements which are open ended statements of intent
⇨ A precise formulation of attribute sought
⇨ A measure of performance towards the attribute
⇨ A clearly defined target to be met
⇨ Have a time frame defined in which attribute is to be achieved
⇨ Are covered by the acronym SMART
⇨ Specific – unambiguous
⇨ Measurable – a quantity
⇨ Attainable
⇨ Relevant – to mission
⇨ Time bound – completion date

Regarding strategic objectives

You should be able to identify appropriate strategic objectives for an organisation, commercial or otherwise. You should also be able to evaluate objectives that an organisation has set for itself. You should be able to distinguish between objectives at the strategic, management and operational level

Remember

Strategic objectives do not have to be quantified in financial terms – but the primary strategic objective usually is (see page 6)

Critical success factors

Critical success factors

'Those components of strategy where the organisation must excel to outperform competition. These are underpinned by competences which ensure success. A critical success factor analysis can be used as a basis for preparing resource plans'

Methodology for CSF analysis

⇨ Identify CSFs for the specified strategic goal
⇨ Identify the essential underpinning competences
⇨ Make sure this list is accurate and sufficient to give competitive advantage

⇨ Identify appropriate performance standards to outperform rivals – Key Performance Indicators (KPIs)
⇨ Ensure that competitive advantage is sustainable and cannot be imitated or acquired
⇨ Monitor competitor performance and predict the impact of their likely reactions to firms strategies

Regarding CSFs

You should make sure that you can identify the critical success factors for any industry that could feature in a scenario. You could get this information from reading the financial times or the business section from another quality daily paper

Objectives for shareholders

Maximising profit

⇨ Traditionally, the objective of the firm is to maximise profit and we see measures such as return on capital employed and earnings per share
⇨ It is only for the current year
⇨ The measures are very short-term
⇨ It ignores risk
⇨ It doesn't represent cash flow available to the shareholder
⇨ They can be manipulated by creative accounting

Maximise shareholder wealth

⇨ Maximisation of present value of free cash flows or
⇨ Maximisation of share price

Worth remembering

If a company has a steadily increasing ROCE, it is worth looking to see if they have been maintaining their capital investment to make the company future-proof

Regarding strategic objectives

You should be able to criticise existing objectives and propose appropriate strategic objectives for a firm

Objectives for not-for-profit organisations

Different types of not-for-profit

⇨ Government departments
⇨ Schools
⇨ Charities

Public sector objectives

⇨ Effectiveness – does it do the job?
⇨ Efficiency – how many tasks does it achieve?
⇨ Economy – the cost of the operation
⇨ Subject to political change

Public sector scrutiny arises because

⇨ Lack of competition
⇨ Lack of profit motive
⇨ Inadequate checks and balances
⇨ Public interest in their performance

Generally for not-for-profits

⇨ Wider stakeholder groups and more of them
⇨ Limited resources
⇨ Have beneficiaries not customers
⇨ Beneficiaries are not normally funders

Objectives for not-for-profit organisations

Please remember

The management of not-for-profit organisations is quite different to the management of commercial organisations and so the decisions they have to make are often made under quite different sets of assumptions and criteria. The importance of a stakeholder analysis for a not-for-profit organisation cannot be stressed enough. The interests of different stakeholder groups often conflict considerably

Regarding not-for-profits

If you are unfamiliar with governmental or other not-for-profit organisations, do spend some time looking at the web sites of these organisations to get a feel for their objectives, mission statements and purpose. Make sure that you have looked at both the example of CIMA in the study manual and questions 2 and 4 in the pilot paper

Competing objectives

Implications of competing objectives

⇨ Development of consistent strategies will need resolution of the conflict
⇨ Choosing between options will be made more difficult by competing objectives
⇨ Similarly, the task of choosing appropriate performance measures will be made harder by competing objectives

Resolution of competing objectives

⇨ Prioritisation – options may have a minimum threshold for one objective before performance against other criteria (or objectives) are considered

⇨ Weighting and scoring – a numerical weighting indicates the relative importance of each objective
⇨ Devise composite measures of performance when implementing and controlling (see the balanced scorecard – described later)

Behavioural approaches

⇨ Satisficing – negotiating between important stakeholders
⇨ Side payments – compensation to those stakeholders whose objectives are not directly met
⇨ Exercise of power – force through the desired option

Appraising the Environment

Key learning system questions

- 2.1 PEST analysis
- 2.2 Porter analysis
- 12 Impact of regulatory regimes
- 13 Impact of regulatory regimes and nature of competitive environments
- 17 Nature of competitive environments
- 19 Impact of regulatory regimes

Topics

- The importance of the business environment
- Causes of environmental uncertainty
- Competitor analysis
- Competitor accounting and sources of information
- The economic environment
- The domestic economy
- National competitive advantage
- Sources of environmental information

The importance of the business environment

Environmental impact assessment

'A study which considers potential environmental effects during the planning phase before an investment is made or an operation started'

Environmental segmentation

⇨ Think of the environment as everything outside the firm and it's control
⇨ We use two main models – Porter Five Forces Analysis. And PEST

Porter Five Forces are

⇨ Rivalry amongst existing firms
⇨ Bargaining power of buyers
⇨ Bargaining power of suppliers
⇨ Threat of new entrants
⇨ Threat of substitute products or services

The value net

One of the criticisms of Porter's model is that it ignores any cooperation between suppliers, buyers and the company itself. This increases the forces in the competitive environment – look out for complementors, where the efforts of one organisation complement the activities of others

Regarding Porters Five Forces

You will have studied this for P5 Integrated Management but it is also examinable at this level. It is an important consideration for any company making decisions about the future of the industry in which they operate. It must be remembered that this is an analytical model and not a descriptive one. It is of no use in just listing the buyers – you must judge how powerful they are

Debate about PEST

Remember that there is a debate about the model that is used. Some authors advocate PESTEL where the 'extra' letters separate out ecological and legal factors. In real companies it doesn't really matter which acronym is used – but it does matter that the company does perform environmental screening. In real life it is difficult to categorise factors as fitting purely into one of the categories of the model. For instance globalisation is an important factor – but is it political, economic or sociological? In fact it has elements of all three and some technological aspects as well

PEST analysis – factors are

⇨ Political /legal influences
⇨ Economic factors and influences
⇨ Social values and demographic factors
⇨ Technological change and factors

Evaluation of environmental segment models

⇨ They will encourage management to consider a wide range of environmental factors
⇨ They allow the division of work between different groups
⇨ They provide a common language for discussion
⇨ They can assist in providing insight into strategic issues
⇨ But they don't reflect reality
⇨ But they ignore the fact that the environment is a complex adaptive system with many interdependencies
⇨ But they may cause management to overlook networks
⇨ They can involve a lot of work

Regarding environmental analysis

Do not just learn one model – you may be asked to compare them. Do make sure that you are aware of the kind of factors that could arise under each category factor. Do practice environmental screening yourself by looking at an industry (or industries) of your choice and see what a company could gain by being more aware of the factors that could bring about change and the elements that make the industry more or less competitive

Whilst you are considering environmental analysis, you should also think about political risk at both the country and industry level. Some governments may seem to penalise particular industries for ideological reasons

Causes of environmental uncertainty

Uncertainty

'The inability to predict the outcome from an activity due to a lack of information about the required input/output relationships or about the environment within which the activity takes place.' Uncertainty can also be defined as 'the difficulty in making reliable assumptions about the future'

Uncertainty caused by

⇨ Complexity – the increasing number of variables that impact upon the firm (and how difficult they are to understand)

⇨ Interaction of the variables – the idea of complex adaptive systems

⇨ Dynamism – the rate of change in the variables that impact upon the firm. Our assumptions are soon out of date. This has occurred because of, amongst other things, shortening product life cycles and swifter communications (the diffusion of knowledge)

Impact of uncertainty

⇨ Reduces planning horizon
⇨ Discourages deliberate strategies
⇨ Increases information needs and perceived information needs
⇨ Can lead to conservative strategies

Regarding uncertainty

You will certainly be presented with uncertainty in examination questions. Please make sure that you can advise the decision makers in the question how to deal with it

Competitor analysis

Competitor analysis

'The systematic review of all available information (marketing, production, financial, etc.) on the activities of competitors in order to gain a competitive advantage'

Purpose of competitor analysis

⇨ To help understanding our competitive advantage/ disadvantage relative to competition
⇨ To forecast competitors future strategies and how to counteract them
⇨ To give an informed basis for the construction of the firms' strategies to gain or sustain competitive advantage
⇨ To assist with the forecasting of the returns on strategic investments when deciding between alternative options

⇨ To forecast competitor's likely reactions to the firms strategic decisions

Competitor threat

We can, and should, tie this back to Five Forces Analysis and the extent to which competitors are a threat depends on

1. Number of rivals and the extent of differentiation in the market – a market for commodity products is always more fiercely competitive
2. Entry and mobility barriers
3. Cost structure – anything that makes it harder to make a profit will make it more fiercely competitive
4. Degree of vertical integration – vertical integration gives power – but removes flexibility

Competitor analysis

A process for gathering competitive intelligence

⇨ Identify competitor's current strategy
⇨ Identify competitor's objectives
⇨ Identify competitor's assumptions about the industry/market
⇨ Identify competitors resources and capabilities

Information that should be gathered

To include: Products and services, Marketing, Human resources, Operations, Management profiles, Sociopolitical, Technology, Organisational structure, Competitive intelligence capacity, Strategy, Customer value analysis, Financial, Cost structures

Regarding competitor analysis

Make sure that you are able to discuss the advantages and disadvantages of competitor analysis – don't forget it is strongly linked to Five Forces Analysis. In scenario questions, you should be looking for clues to the industry structure and therefore, the nature of the competition that a firm is likely to experience in that industry. You should also be able to describe a process for gathering competitive intelligence including the sources you would use tailored to the scenario of the question

Sources of data

⇨ From partnership agreements
⇨ Physical analysis of competitors' products
⇨ Banks and financial markets
⇨ Ex-employees of competitors
⇨ Generalisation from own cost base
⇨ Industrial experts and consultants
⇨ Physical observations of their operations
⇨ Published financial statements
⇨ Competitor press releases
⇨ Trade and financial media coverage
⇨ Inspection of wage rates in job adverts
⇨ Availability and cost of their finance
⇨ Characteristics of the market segments they serve
⇨ The work methods they employ

Regarding sources of data

When presented with a question that looks for sources of information check to see if the question asks you to relate it to the scenario in the question – if it does don't just put down a wish list, focus on the industry in question

The economic environment

We need to consider the economic environment at two levels:

1. The global economic environment
2. The operational economic environment in the country or countries in which the firm operates

The global economic environment

⇨ An important trend is internationalisation – the extension of trade across national borders
⇨ A further important trend is globalisation – the functional integration of internationally dispersed activities

Globalisation is being brought about by

⇨ Extension of supply chains across national boundaries
⇨ Changing patterns of foreign direct investment (FDI)
⇨ The creation of supranational organisations
⇨ Economic changes being driven by technology
⇨ The spread of multinational enterprises
⇨ Transfer of particular industries across national boundaries causing the spread of dominant cultures and lifestyles

Regulatory bodies

With the rise of globalisation we see the possibility of:

1. Blue collar unemployment in developed countries
2. Increased outsourcing
3. Defensive national government policies
4. Pressure for global governance

Regional economic blocks

There are a number of economic or trade blocks which play an important part in the economic environment of the firm. They are increasingly exercising their power in an attempt to control powerful multinational companies.

The European Union and NAFTA are two such bodies but there are others. Generally their scope covers:

1. Regional policy and cross border cooperation
2. Agriculture, fisheries and rural development
3. Infrastructure and the information society
4. The environment, energy policy and spatial planning
5. Social policy, consumer protection and tourism
6. Employment, economic policy regarding single markets, industry, small and medium sized enterprises
7. Education, vocational training culture and citizen's rights

Any company with international aspirations must consider the impact of these bodies seriously together with a consideration of the World Trade Organisation and the World Bank

The economic environment

Regarding global economics

Make sure that you are aware of the influence that these bodies EU, NAFTA, WTO, etc. could have any decisions that you are asked to make on behalf of a firm in a question

Objectives of macroeconomic policy

⇨ Promote a high and stable level of employment
⇨ Maintain price stability with no, or controlled, inflation
⇨ Maintain equilibrium in the balance of payments
⇨ Promote economic growth
⇨ Enhance the material standard of living of the population

No government can achieve all of these together – it is impossible. There will be a political judgement about the point at which a balance should be struck. The economy will go through 'a business cycle' and there will be policy decisions made by the government at the various stages of that cycle to achieve their objectives

This assumes that the appropriate unit of macroeconomic policy is the nation state which is in doubt because:

1. The increased role of international capital markets
2. The development of multinational markets
3. The creation of pan – national economic and political bodies
4. The global trend to free trade

Regarding domestic and global economies

Make sure that you know what policy reactions governments may make at various stages of the business cycle to try and achieve their chosen balance between the objectives above. Also make sure you know what that can mean to a firm and the economic environment it faces

National competitive advantage

Porter's diamond

Attempts to answer the questions:

Why do certain nations have so many successful international firms?

How do these firms sustain superior performance in a global market?

What are the implications of this for government policy and competitive strategy?

The elements of success are:

⇨ Demand conditions in the home market gives the firm a strong base and the opportunity to fund research and development

⇨ Related and supporting industries will give a firm access to expertise and a skill base to conduct it's business. The concept of 'clusters' which can occur through geography or expertise in a particular industry or technology

⇨ Factor conditions are needed by the firm to conduct their business – the greater the proportion of advanced factors (sophisticated infrastructure, digital communications, R&D, high training and skill) the greater the chances of the firms success

⇨ The firm's structure, strategy and rivalry will be affected by national cultures and attitude to business. Ownership structures, openness of the market and attitudes of, and to, capital markets will all affect the firm's chances of success

⇨ Additionally, governments can foster an atmosphere which supports firms in their efforts by subsidies, encouraging enterprise and infrastructure building and putting in place an appropriate legislative system

Porter's strategic prescriptions

⇨ The firm should identify which home country clusters will give an advantage – either cost or differentiation

⇨ If those advantages are world class, they should compete on a global basis

⇨ If those advantages are not world class, they should compete locally in an appropriate niche market

Regarding national competitive advantage

By reading widely you should consider why some countries seem to host more successful companies than others. Ask yourself what those countries have done to attract and support those firms? You might want to think what a company would expect from a host nation to encourage them to invest there

Sources of environmental information

Gathering environmental information can be done at different levels of intensity and levels within the organisation:

1. In addition to their operational duties, line management should have the responsibility of environmental scanning in the medium term
2. Those responsible for the strategic planning of the organisation should have the task of gathering information with a longer time horizon
3. There may be 'business intelligence units' whose specific responsibility is scanning

If scanning is done at these levels, it is important that gatherers meet regularly. For instance those with strategic responsibility may miss the weak signals but those at the operational level will see

Importance of environmental scanning

⇨ Provides a base of (hopefully) objective qualitative information
⇨ Assists firm in seizing opportunities and protecting against threats
⇨ Encourages sensitivity to changing needs of society and hence customers
⇨ Provides essential information for strategic planning process
⇨ Provides intellectual stimulation for strategists
⇨ Provides a broad-based education and awareness for managers
⇨ Creates a good impression both inside and outside the firm

Categorisation of sources

⇨ Primary sources such as annual reports, transcript services, government surveys and departments, newspapers, magazines and journals and patent registrations

⇨ Secondary sources such as directories and yearbooks, market research reviews and reports, current awareness services, specialist databases, reports from government committees and conference reports

⇨ Computer-based information (of increasing importance), on line data bases of professional journals and academic institutions, CD Rom-based abstracts and journals

⇨ The Internet in particular

Regarding environmental scanning and information sources

Throughout this chapter, we have discussed the importance of information external to the company and how it can be gathered. Many companies do not take this area as seriously as they should for a variety of reasons – too much effort, too hard, too complicated are amongst the most common quoted

A Management Accountant is ideally placed to gather some of the information and to know what other information that others should gather. You should make sure that you are able to answer questions that take you in this direction

Position Appraisal and Analysis

Key learning system questions

3.2 Value chain analysis
3.3 Benchmarking
3.4 SWOT analysis
  3 Value chain analysis

Topics

- The SWOT analysis
- The position audit
- Value chain analysis
- Benchmarking
- Gap analysis
- Scenario planning

According to CIMA, a SWOT analysis and a corporate appraisal are the same thing, and has also been described as position appraisal. It is designed to enable management to interpret the information they have gathered about the firm and its environment. You should remember that the assumption is that strengths and weaknesses are internal to the firm whilst opportunities and threats are external to the firm. However, internal factors can also be a threat, skill or age profile of the staff for instance, and this is felt to be a weakness of the technique

Corporate appraisal

'A critical assessment of the strengths and weaknesses, opportunities and threats (SWOT analysis) in relation to the internal and environmental factors affecting an entity in order to establish its condition prior to the preparation of the long-term plan'

The popularity of the technique, using a simple 2×2 matrix on a flip chart, is it's simplicity and that the limited space to write forces management to focus on the big issues. The technique could focus management into:

1. Matching – build on strengths to capitalise on opportunities
2. Converting – by reinterpreting weaknesses and threats as opportunities
3. Remedying – curing the weaknesses by appropriate action

The TOWS approach

An alternative approach uses a 3×3 matrix that plots strengths and weaknesses against opportunities and . threats to give four groups of strategies – (S)trength (O)pportunities strategies, WO strategies, ST strategies and WT strategies

The extended matrix offers limited advantage

The value of SWOT (or TOWS)

This is one of the most criticised techniques in strategic management since it is usually difficult to get an objective analysis done. There is often a temptation to produce a 'wish list' rather than an objective comparison against other players in the industry. The earlier point that threats, and for that matter opportunities, can be internal to the firm is also made. Having said that, as long as it is recognised that it is a simple summary, it can be used as a start in a process of more detailed analysis

Regarding SWOT and TOWS

It is highly likely that you will be asked to comment on the strengths and weaknesses of an organisation as part of the answer to a scenario question. If you are, you must be realistic in your answer – do not produce a wish list! It may be that you are not formally asked to produce a SWOT, but are asked to evaluate, or even suggest and evaluate, various options. It would be difficult to do so without considering the capabilities of the company – you'll need to do a SWOT to do so

Arguably this is a more rigorous form of analysis than the SWOT analysis – or should be

The position audit

Part of the planning process which examines the current state of the entity in respect of:

1. Resources of tangible and intangible assets and finance
2. Products, brands and markets
3. Operating systems such as production and distribution
4. Internal organisation
5. Current results
6. Returns to stockholders

This is not an exhaustive list and there are other factors that can, and should be considered. The 'M's model will give an indication of this

The 'M's model

⇨ Men – human assets in terms of skill profile, morale and age profile
⇨ Management – quality, expertise and experience of top team
⇨ Money – financial health and quality of relationship with banks and shareholders
⇨ Make-up-appropriateness of organisational structure and culture of firm
⇨ Machinery – flexibility and relative cost of the physical assets of the business
⇨ Markets – the firms products and their position in the markets they serve
⇨ Materials – the quality of the relationship with suppliers, 'partnership' or diversity of suppliers are considerations here
⇨ Management information – quality and timeliness of information for decision making particularly, the breadth of the information and the intelligibility

The position audit

Conducting the position audit

The position audit must consider all information that can impact upon performance – both under present strategies and proposed changes to strategies. Although normally conducted by multidisciplinary team, management accountants should play a significant role. First, they should provide information on the cost and financial situation of the firm now and forecasts of what it could (and should) be in the future. Second, working with other functional specialists to determine the financial impacts of the information that they have gathered

Regarding position audits

As with SWOT analysis, it is highly likely that you will be required, particularly with scenario questions, to produce a position audit. You will almost certainly be expected to do this from the perspective of a multidisciplinary team – make sure you know what the other functional experts ought to look for!

There are a number of other techniques that can be used for analysing the strengths and weaknesses of organisations. We will review them over the next few pages

Value chain analysis

Possibly one of the most powerful techniques for analysing the strengths and weaknesses of an organisation and it's component functions, value chain analysis can be used to compare those features with other organisations. The model can be used at varying degrees in sophistication from purely qualitatively and descriptively to fully quantified, often financially. The model, developed by Michael Porter looks at the functions within an organisation to determine where value is added either by cost leadership or differentiation – the only two routes to competitive advantage (according to Porter)

The value chain

'The sequence of business activities by which, in the perspective of the end user, value is added to the products and/or services produced by the organisation.' 'A systematic way of examining all the activities a firm performs and how they interact ... (the value chain) desegregates a firm into its strategically relevant activities in order to understand the behaviour of costs and the existing and potential sources of differentiation'

Value chain analysis

Manufacturing value chain

There are five primary activities, which are:

⇨ Inbound logistics – receipt and handling of inputs to process
⇨ Operations – conversion of inputs to outputs
⇨ Outbound logistics – storing and distribution of outputs to customers
⇨ Marketing and sales – providing customers with the information, incentive and means to buy the products
⇨ Service – after-sales service to enhance and maintain the value of the product

There are four support activities, which are:

⇨ Procurement – purchasing of inputs and business services needed by the firm
⇨ Technology development – very broad category covering product research, process research but also things like marketing research
⇨ Human resource management – recruitment, training, development, retention and discharge of staff – must include succession planning
⇨ Firm's infrastructure – general management, accounting finance, legal, information systems, basically the support functions

Value chain analysis

Porter argues that by considering these functions as support activities rather than grouping them together as overhead we are better able to determine where they add value. It is important to consider linkages within the value chain – the primary activities do not function in isolation nor do the support activities. As we shall see later, when we discuss business process re-engineering these relationships and how the firms infrastructure manages them are an important source of competitive advantage

It is also important to consider vertical linkages in the industry value system. You might care to think that the outbound logistics of your supplier is strongly linked to your own inbound logistics – by cooperating you both may gain competitive advantage. This is the basis of supply chain partnerships (which we will discuss later) and the Value Net – as we discussed earlier. With this in mind it is important for a firm to conduct an industry

value system analysis. Thinking of the whole industry from raw materials to final end user as a progression of individual value chains – which stages in the value system enjoy the largest margins? Is the firm capable of working at that stage of the industry?

Management accounting and the value chain

Note the similarity between this approach and that taken in activity-based costing where department boundaries are ignored. In a deep and rigorous application this becomes strategic cost analysis which has the following steps:

⇨ Identify the activities conducted by the business units and groups within the value chain categories
⇨ Determine the cost incurred by conducting each activity

Value chain analysis

⇨ Identify opportunities to either reduce costs without reducing customer perceived value or, by enhancing perceived value give an opportunity to increase costs

Look at the example in the Learning System in Section 3.3.9 of the Study Manual

Alternative value chains

To counter some of the claims that the original value chain is only appropriate to manufacturing organisations, other models have been developed. In the following two examples the support activities remain the same but the primary activities are different

Professional services value chain

There are five primary activities, which are:

⇨ Problem acquisition and diagnosis – persuading clients to bring issues to the firm and determining the exact nature of the problem

⇨ Finding potential solutions – using professional expertise and knowledge base of the firm

⇨ Choice between possible solutions – either making the choice or facilitating the client, making the choice

⇨ Implementing the chosen solution

⇨ Control and feedback – monitoring the effect of the solution to ensure the desired outcome

Network organisation value chain

⇨ Network promotion and contract management – finding clients and management of service providers, effectively the management of contractors

⇨ Service provisioning – day to day operation of the network, billing, tracking usage of the service

⇨ Infrastructure operation – keeping the network maintained and functional

Value chain analysis

It is worth noting at this point that value chains can be modified to suit the organisation being analysed – there is no hard and fast rule about the 'shape' of an organisation. Similarly, for manufacturing value chains, the primary activities are not necessarily performed in the order represented in the diagram in the manual. For instance, if a firm is making to order, marketing would almost certainly come 'before' operations

Evaluating value chain analysis

⇨ Has had a profound effect on management thinking
⇨ An effective way to analyse a firm in terms of the processes it uses to serve its customers
⇨ A good framework to use, to analyse competitors

⇨ Provides a common terminology for management when conducting an analysis of strengths and weaknesses
⇨ A basis for other management techniques such as: benchmarking, business process re-engineering, activity-based costing, information systems strategy, analysis of transaction costs and decisions about outsourcing
⇨ Can indicate a route to generating superior competitive advantage
⇨ A basis for developing performance measures
⇨ But managers can find its application complex
⇨ It can be an expensive exercise to conduct in great detail
⇨ Has been criticised because it is linear and ignores value networks

Value chain analysis

Regarding value chain analysis

Since a value chain analysis is one of the best approaches to strengths and weaknesses analysis, you may well find yourself having to do this in the examination. It is something you can practice, at the descriptive level, by looking at real organisations that you know or are aware of from your broader reading. Don't forget to consider the linkages between the activities, which can be just as important as the activities themselves. Try applying a professional services value chain to a not-for-profit organisation

Supply chain management

'The supply chain is the network of organisations that are involved, through upstream and downstream linkages, in the different processes and activities that produce value in the form of products and services in the hands of the ultimate consumer'

Please note that this is different to supply management, which relates solely to goods inwards. Supply chain management is concerned with the whole chain and considers not only the logistics but also the relationships between the organisations. Logistics management is concerned with such issues as: procurement management, materials movement and storage, inventory management both finished goods and raw materials together with the management of distribution channels. Supply chain management has become important because of:

1. The customer services explosion – expectations of service excellence have been raised
2. Time compression – shorter product life cycles and more frequent new product development because of customer sophistication
3. Globalisation of industry – multinational operations involve a complex web of international transactions involving materials, components and finished goods
4. Organisational integration – many more organisations work as teams and in partnerships with their suppliers and buyers

Supply chain management has three main themes: responsiveness, reliability and relationships. (you might want to remember this when we discuss relationship marketing)

Implementing supply chain management

1. Create a logistics vision – decide how logistics strength can be used to deliver perceived value to the customer
2. Develop the logistics organisation – build a 'horizontal organisation' that focuses on the customer
3. Increase integration – across the organisation and across the upstream and downstream linkages
4. Manage the supply chain as a network – get rid of the 'us and them' mentality, introduce collective strategy development, win–win thinking and open communications

Benchmarking

Benchmarking

'The establishment, through data gathering, of targets and comparators, through whose use relative levels of performance (and particularly areas of underperformance) can be identified. By the adoption of identified best practices it is hoped that performance will improve'

Internal benchmarking – comparing one operating unit or function with another within the same industry

Functional benchmarking – internal functions are compared with the performance of the best practitioners of those functions, regardless of industry or organisation

Competitive benchmarking – comparison with direct competitors

Strategic benchmarking – gathering information to assist in strategic action and organisational change

Setting up a benchmarking exercise

1. Gain senior management commitment to the benchmarking project – ensures cooperation and commitment further down the organisation
2. Decide the processes and activities to be benchmarked – start by identifying outcomes that drive profits and work backwards
3. Understand the process and develop appropriate measures – by discussion and observation
4. Monitor the process measurement system – look for reliability in data capture and reliability of the data itself
5. Choose appropriate organisations against which to benchmark (see list under definitions)
6. Obtain and analyse data
7. Discuss results with process management and staff – should be a 'blame free' process

8. Develop and implement improvement programmes – benchmarking itself will not improve things, it can only provide the evidence so to do
9. Monitor results – by its nature benchmarking is not a one-off process but an element in a continuous improvement process

Evaluation of benchmarking

⇨ Can help to improve organisational performance
⇨ Can assist in overcoming complacency
⇨ Can help bring about organisational change
⇨ Can provide a means of monitoring the conduct of strategic plans
⇨ Can provide a warning of deteriorating competitive position

⇨ Can provide management with a better understanding of the value adding processes of the firm
⇨ But may overload management with information
⇨ But may reduce management motivation when benchmarked against a 'better' resourced rival
⇨ But can lead to focus on existing business at expense of new business. 'Benchmarking is the refuge of the manager who is afraid of the future'
⇨ But may breach confidentiality of proprietary data
⇨ But can increase the cost of control

Regarding benchmarking

Apart from being asked to discuss benchmarking and its pros and cons it is also possible that you might be asked to conduct a benchmarking exercise. (You should always aim to tie your answer into the situation in the question anyway.) Spend some time think about processes in organisations and who it might be possible, and wise, to benchmark them against. Additionally you should look at the stages in the 'introduction of a benchmarking exercise' above. This is a fairly good example of the stages involved in the introduction of anything new in an organisation and, with a bit of adaption might help you answer a question about a different process that has to be introduced into a firm

Gap analysis

Gap analysis

A comparison between an entity's ultimate objective
(most commonly expressed in terms of demand,
but may be in terms of profit, ROCE, etc.) and the
expected aggregate performance of projects both
planned and under way. Differences are classified
in a way which aids the understanding of
performance, and which facilitates improvement

Forecasts and projections

'A projection is – an expected future trend
pattern obtained by extrapolation. It is principally
concerned with quantitative factors, whereas a
forecast includes judgements'

'A forecast is – a prediction of future events and
their quantification for planning purposes'

Literally, a comparison between where the organisation
wants to be and where it will be if it makes no changes,
'does nothing,' to it's current operations and plans. Once
the gap is established then various strategic options can
be considered as possible means to close the remaining
performance gap

Gap analysis depends on the organisations ability to
forecast and make projections

One of the problems with forecasting and, indeed, one of
the reasons for the decline in popularity of gap analysis
is the problem of uncertainty on which some arguement
has been increasing. It is argued that there are four
levels of uncertainty

Gap analysis

Levels of uncertainty

⇨ A clear enough future – a stable environment, single forecasts can be developed

⇨ Alternative futures – it may be possible to assign probabilities to different outcomes

⇨ A range of futures – a desired outcome may take a range of possible outcomes. It is no longer possible to visualise two or even three outcomes and assign probabilities. Modelling may be done to attempt to get a feel for the possible outcomes. High low forecasts, What if? analysis and simulation models are amongst the techniques that may be used

⇨ True ambiguity – where the environment is virtually impossible to predict

⇨ As we progress down this list, the feasibility of 'rational planning' declines and organisational flexibility becomes more and more important

⇨ One of the approaches to dealing with uncertainty and developing organisational flexibility is scenario planning

Scenario planning

Scenarios are stories about the future used to change managers mind sets to encourage them to think expansively about what the future may hold. They can be used in strategy formulation as follows:

1. Develop scenarios about the external environment and identify key trends and uncertainties
2. Conduct industry analysis to determine what the industry structure could look like if either scenario comes true
3. Identify core capabilities of the firm and develop strategies that are robust under either scenario
4. Adopt the appropriate strategic option and adapt as the future, which is now better understood, unfolds

Constructing scenarios

There is no one correct way to construct scenarios but the following offers one of the more popular approaches:

1. Define the scope of the scenarios – time frame and definition of industry
2. Identify stakeholders and drivers of change – which stakeholders are likely to drive change?
3. Identify basic trends – these will often be things about which the firm is fairly certain within the time frame chosen
4. Identify key uncertainties – the factors that will influence the way things develop
5. Construct initial scenarios themes – combine assumptions about uncertainties

6. Check for internal consistency and plausibility – do they make sense in the time frame suggested?
7. Develop learning scenarios – flesh out the stories into believable and convincing pictures of the future
8. Identify research needs – decide what information needs to be gathered to fill in the gaps in the firm's knowledge highlighted by the scenarios
9. Develop quantitative models – sometimes possible to quantify the outcomes of each scenario, but not always possible or realistic
10. Develop courses of action that are equally robust under both scenarios

Strategic Aspects of Marketing

This chapter will examine the sources of a firm's revenues and profit, its products and customers

Topics

- Sources of earnings
- Product life cycles
- Portfolio models
- Direct product profitability
- The marketing audit
- Customer profitability analysis
- Brands and brand strategies
- Relationship marketing
- Data warehousing and data mining

Key learning system questions

4.2 Customer account profitability
4.5 Product profitability analysis

Sources of earnings

We can make the assumption that earnings are generated by products and then use techniques such as direct product profitability and/or product profitability analysis. Or we can consider that customers are the source of earnings and use customer account profitability. We can also consider the earnings generated by a product throughout it's life – life cycle profitability

Remember

You may be asked to apply all of these techniques so please make sure you are fully familiar and practised with all of them

Product life cycles

The product life cycle model

There are similarities between the industry life cycle, which we discussed earlier, and the product life cycle. The model suggests that a product passes through the following stages: introduction, growth, shake-out, maturity and finally decline. It is argued that by identifying the stage of their products in the life cycle a firm may be able to predict the behaviour of their rivals and make decisions about what action they, themselves, should take. Additionally, at different stages of the product life cycle, because of the different characteristics of the market different profit measures may be appropriate

Criticism of the product life cycle model

⇨ There is a lack of clarity about the level at which the model works – industry, product category, product type, brand?

⇨ It is not possible to forecast precisely when the various stages will start and end – it is a descriptive model

⇨ It focuses on the product rather than on the market

⇨ It assumes that the stages are inevitable – they may not be, or may be prolonged by management efforts

⇨ It fails to consider complementary products

Portfolio models

Portfolio models are used to assist in the management of the organisation as a collection of income yielding assets. As such, the models can be used at a product level or at the level of strategic business units (SBU's)

The most well-known of these models is the Boston Consulting Group matrix – BCG matrix, which plots products (or SBU's) against two axes:

⇨ Relative market share
⇨ Market growth rate

The model was developed to be prescriptive and, depending on the position in the matrix, products were classified as: stars (high market share/strong market growth), cash cows (high market share/weak market growth), dogs (low market share/weak market growth) or problem children (low market share/strong market growth). The prescriptions were that stars should be supported, cash cows should be milked, dogs should be divested and problem children should be divested or, if sufficient funds were available, grown into stars

The importance of relative market share

It must be remembered that the BCG is old and at the time of its development the concept of experience curves was very popular with the result that it was believed market domination was essential for low costs and thereby competitive success

Alternative portfolio models

The model has been adapted to consider the attractiveness of customers rather than products – with some modification to the axes

The Mckinsey Group produced an alternative model with composite axes

The relative market share became business strength factors and a weighted score was calculated for each SBU

Portfolio models

Market growth rate became industry attractiveness factors and again a weighted score was calculated

The matrix, which had nine cells instead of the four for the BCG, was again prescriptive resulting in decisions such as, invest to rebuild, selective investment, low investment, divestment

Criticisms of portfolio models

⇨ The experience curve is, to a large extent, discredited – so the rationale behind the model is faulty

⇨ There are, invariably, problems with defining the market – there are rarely 'pure' markets for products

⇨ With the exception of the McKinsey model, the axes are too simplistic (the McKinsey axes are argued to be too subjective)

⇨ The technique ignores complementary products

⇨ Prescriptive models are not a great help to innovative strategic management

⇨ The prescription are sometimes wrong – some companies make a good living from being the supplier of last resort – selling products classified as dogs

⇨ Companies can be lulled into a sense of complacency – and the model only considers the demand side of the firm

Regarding portfolio models

In general, this chapter has been critical of portfolio models and you should make sure that you are able to evaluate them. They do have the benefit of being able to demonstrate, in a fairly simple form, the strengths and weaknesses of the firm's product portfolio as such they may be useful to you if you find yourself evaluating a firm's business in a scenario question

Direct product profitability

Direct product profitability

'… the attribution of costs other than the purchase price (e.g. distribution, warehousing, retailing) to each product line. Thus a net profit, as opposed to a gross profit, can be identified for each product …'

Today most retailers will calculate DPP for themselves, in the past suppliers have calculatd DPP to use in bargaining sessions with customers and to better understand how to convince a retailer to carry more stock

Calculating DPP

1. Establish the determinants of sales revenue – price of the product, frequency with which it is purchased and the amount of sales returns generated

2. Establish the determinants of costs – this has been the most useful aspect of DPP. Cost to the retailer can include: unit price charged by supplier, costs of placing the order, inventory and storage costs, transport costs from warehouse to the store, costs of shelf filling together with wastage and breakage costs

3. The DPP analysis will break down costs to determine drivers, for instance, for stock holding drivers might well be: the size of the product, the uncertainty of demand, the delivery cycle and the ordering method. A rigorous ABC analysis will be necessary to get full benefit from the exercise

Improving DPP

DPP can be improved by any of the following:

1. Increase the final sales price of the product
2. Increase the sales volume of the product
3. Reduce the cost of selling the product – reduce it's physical dimensions, increase frequency of deliveries to reduce stock holding, improve sales forecasting to optimise inventory
4. Provide incentives to retailers to stock product

Evaluation of DPP

⇨ The technique can encourage management to become product led rather than marketing led
⇨ Costs of a DPP exercise may be greater than the loss of profit from a discount to retailers
⇨ Ignores complementary products – which could lead to knock on losses of sales if a product is abandoned

The marketing audit

Marketing audit

'A particular form of position audit that focuses on the products of the firm and the relationship it has with its customers'

A refresher on marketing

You should revise the work you did for *Organisational Management and Information Systems* from which you should remember the basic principles of marketing. Remember that, from the perspective of marketing, firms are in the business of satisfying needs. According to

Kotler the marketing concept is based on four pillars:

⇨ Target markets – segmentation of markets is important and effective

⇨ Needs and benefits – the importance of marketing research in deciding what these are before a product is developed and marketed, cannot be over emphasised

⇨ Integrated marketing – determining the appropriate combination of the marketing mix

⇨ Profitability – will arise from satisfying the needs and wants of valuable customer segments

The marketing mix that is referred to consists of:

⇨ Product – physical features of the offering

⇨ Price – terms on which the purchase is made

⇨ Promotion – message and media by which it is conveyed

⇨ Place – the distribution channels used

Steps in a marketing audit

⇨ Define the market – benefits the firm seeks to deliver and the key characteristics of the market, size, growth rate and a statement of the key requirements for success in the chosen market

⇨ Determine performance differentials – identification of subsectors or niches where an entry to the market can be made. Evaluate market in general but also look at differences in performance of main competitors

⇨ Determine the differences in competitive programmes – what marketing strategies are being used by competitors and how might they change in the future? Effectively conduct a position audit on the competitor firms

⇨ Profile the strategies of competitors – profile each significant competitor or strategic approach and decide how to counter

⇨ Determine the strategic planning structure – make decisions about how the firm's effort will be structured and organised

Regarding marketing and marketing audits

First, you must make sure that you have revised and are fully familiar with the concepts of marketing that you have successfully learned for earlier papers in the qualification. The examiner will make the assumption that you have retained this knowledge. Regarding marketing audits, specifically you could be asked to explain how to conduct one for a firm or, given sufficient information within a long scenario question, you could be asked to perform one yourself

Customer profitability analysis

Customer profitability analysis

'Analysis of the revenue streams and service costs associated with specific customers or customer groups'

A profitable customer is defined, by Kotler, as 'A person, household or company that, over time, yields a revenue stream that exceeds by an acceptable amount the company's cost stream of attracting, selling and servicing that customer'

Remember

There are two views of customer profitability analysis implied by these definitions – the first suggest analysis on a single period basis, the second infers that analysis can be done on a life cycle basis – both are equally useful and examinable

Customer account profitability (CAP) analysis

This takes the single period view of the value of the customer. The approach would be as follows:

1. Analyse the customer base and divide into segments – regardless of the segmentation done by the marketing department this should be done on the basis of impact upon costs and revenues. For instance, this could be on the basis of annual purchase volume, average size of order, method of ordering, mix of products bought, degree of customer support demanded or payment method used

2. Calculate the annual revenues earned from these customer segments – this should take into account any discounts granted or costs of customisation

3. Calculate the annual costs of serving those segments – this will involve a rigorous analysis of the firms overheads as well as the direct costs. This could include: costs of order getting, customisation costs, promotional costs to the segment, number of delivery drops, location of customer, returns, warranties or refunds

4. Identify and retain the quality customers

5. Eliminate or re-engineer those customer groups who are unprofitable – cease to supply by increasing prices (or charges) or change the variables that make the account unprofitable. This could include, increasing minimum order size, introduce on-line ordering for small customers, charging for order handling or, put up prices generally, whilst giving a discount for bulk orders

Attribute costing

This is CAP analysis, taken a step further, and has the advantage of being more marketing oriented since it focuses less on the product and more on product attributes. The marketing view is that customers perceive a product as a collection of attributes (or benefits) rather than just as a product. The steps in an attribute costing exercise are:

1. List separately the product benefits offered to the customers – must be done from the customers' perspective and with the purchasing decision process in mind

2. Decide on a set of cost categories for the product – Bromwich suggested a set of categories modified from activity-based costing. These were: product volume related, activity related, capacity related and decision related. Using the value chain approach (we discussed earlier) costs should be assigned to activities and the cost of achieving key performance indicators for those activities determined

3. Calculate the value of offering those product attributes – for instance if we consider speed of delivery. Compare our profitability with that of a rival for the respective levels of service provided – would the customers value the change we could offer sufficiently to increase our profitability?

4. Redesign marketing offering to enhance overall profitability this could be done by value engineering, by augmenting existing products with additional features and benefits or by target pricing

Evaluation of CAP analysis

⇨ It takes into account non-production costs in determining profitability
⇨ It provides a method of identifying customer groups who are valuable and worth retaining
⇨ It provides a method of assessing the financial value of the marketing effort and product development expenditures
⇨ However, it can lead to ill judged product modifications
⇨ The practical application is extremely time consuming and difficult
⇨ It may overlook the complementary nature of products offered
⇨ It does not consider the life cycle value of a product or customer, which may be considerable

Life cycle customer value

This involves estimating the present value of the revenues likely to arise from a customer group and comparing them to the life cycle costs of attracting, retaining and servicing that customer group

The approach is complex to apply and, as with all long-term decision making, is heavily dependent upon the quality of the assumptions made at the outset

Regarding customer profitability analysis

This is very much a technique for strategic evaluation – it has no place in short-term control. You should be fully aware of the advantages and disadvantages of the approaches given here and ensure that you could make the appropriate calculations if asked to do so

Description of a brand

1. A name or logo
2. A colour scheme, packaging, livery or 'get-up' – something distinctive and instantly recognisable
3. Associations – features which will appeal to the target market segment, these would include;
   (i) Attributes – such as quality or originality
   (ii) Benefits – such as wealth or credibility
   (iii) Values – such as safety or environmentalism
   (iv) Culture – such as design or technical sophistication
   (v) Personality – people the customer would like to associate with
   (vi) User – the kind of person who ought to buy the product

Importance of brands

Brands are particularly important at the strategic level of the organisation because:

1. Brands may be a better unit of financial analysis
2. Brands should have a longer life cycle than an individual product
3. The concept and understanding of brands is essential to determine the value of a product range
4. The strength of a brand will facilitate market entry in new markets or market segments
5. Powerful brands build a psychological switching cost and reduce buyer power

There are arguments against the power of brands and this is most common in the retail sector where supermarket 'own brands' have had a considerable impact

Branding strategies

The following branding strategies have been suggested by Kotler:

⇨ Line extensions or branded variants
⇨ Brand extensions
⇨ Multibrands
⇨ New brands
⇨ Co-brands

Regarding brand strategies

Make sure that you revise the advantages and disadvantages of each of these strategies and that you could apply the concept to a company described in a scenario

Financial management of brands

Various approaches have been suggested to the valuation of brands:

⇨ The aggregate cost of all of the research and development and marketing expenditure on the brand over a specified period of time
⇨ A valuation based on the present value of the price premium that the brand can command over the unbranded good
⇨ Valuation at market value, effectively the premium that could be charged were the brand to be auctioned off
⇨ A valuation based on consumer-based measures such as esteem, recognition or awareness
⇨ Valuation based on the present value of future earnings potential

Brands and brand strategies

Putting a value on brands has three potential benefits to the firm:

⇨ Can be included on the balance sheet as part of the net assets – giving a true representation of worthy and reducing the capital gearing levels

⇨ Would enable the firm to use investment appraisal techniques to evaluate brand support expenditure

⇨ Would provide a performance indicator to assist in brand management decisions

Regarding valuation of brands

Make sure you can discuss how to do it and why a company would want to, together with the advantages and disadvantages of doing so

Relationship marketing

Relationship marketing is the devoting of marketing resources to maintaining and exploiting the firm's existing customer base rather than the use of resources solely to attract new customers

Contrast with traditional marketing

It is claimed that relationship marketing differs from traditional marketing in that:

⇨ There is a focus on customer retention and loyalty
⇨ An increased emphasis on product benefits that are meaningful to the customer

⇨ It employs longer timescales, recognising that short-term costs may be higher, but so will long-term profits
⇨ Has an emphasis on higher levels of customer service – possibly tailored to individual customers
⇨ Involves a higher customer commitment
⇨ Involves closer customer contact with each contact being used to gather information and build the relationship
⇨ Recognises the importance of quality in all aspects of dealings with customers

It has been suggested that there is a broader role for relationship marketing – rather than just the traditional customer – the six markets model summarises this:

⇨ Customer markets – buyers of the final product

Relationship marketing

⇨ Referral markets – institutions and individuals who could, as intermediaries, refer customers to the firm
⇨ Supplier markets – collaborative partnerships to improve performance (think back to supply chain management discussed earlier)
⇨ Recruitment markets – sources of good staff, who will treat customers well re-enforcing the relationship marketing concept
⇨ Influence markets – those who have influence over purchases and customers for example, regulators and pressure groups
⇨ Internal markets – the relationship between departments within a firm can have a knock-on effect on the customer. Many departments are, effectively, customers of each other

Developing relationship marketing

There are a number of steps necessary to develop a relationship marketing approach within the firm:

⇨ Ensure senior management commitment and endorsement
⇨ Develop incentive schemes to encourage appropriate action from staff
⇨ Reduce staff turnover so that relationships can form
⇨ Adopt quality procedures which monitor and influence all aspects of customer relationship
⇨ Monitor and track customer relationship and make appropriate changes
⇨ Develop detailed information on customer's relationships and buying habits – inform all staff
⇨ Develop strategies to encourage customer loyalty

Regarding relationship marketing

Whilst you could be asked directly to comment on relationship marketing and what it entails, you might find that it is something you wish to suggest to remedy a problem that a firm is experiencing in a question

Data warehousing and data mining

Data warehousing

Data warehousing is aimed at addressing two organisational needs:

⇨ The requirement for collated, organisational wide, information

⇨ The need for the information systems department to manage information in an effective and efficient manner

As such data warehousing has become a very important feature of decision support systems

A data warehouse

Is a database that:

Is organised to serve as a neutral data storage area

Is used by data mining and other applications

Meets a specific set of business requirements

Uses data that meets a predefined set of business criteria

A data warehouse is, effectively, a large relational database collating data, which is continuously updated, from a variety of sources

Currently a data warehouse is likely to satisfy three primary functions:

⇨ Presentation of standard reports and graphs of data consolidated from a variety of diverse sources
⇨ Supporting dimensional analysis by a query and reporting function across a variety of dimensions – particularly time periods
⇨ Enabling the process of data mining

Data mining

Data mining is concerned with the discovery of new meaningful information so that the decision makers in a firm can make the maximum use of the valuable data assets held within the firm. The technique searches for hidden relationships, patterns, correlations and interdependencies in the data that, it is hoped, will lead to competitive advantage. Various statistical and modelling techniques are used to determine these relationships ranging from simple spreadsheets to artificial intelligence programmes. There is always pressure for the firm to gain a competitive advantage – and that pressure is very strong in the area of data mining and warehousing aided by the advances being made in computer technology

Objectives and management issues

As with all projects, successful investment in data warehousing and mining needs clear objectives and a good understanding of the critical success factors of the organisation. The objectives could include:

⇨ To support strategic decision making
⇨ To support an integrated business value chain
⇨ To speed up response time to business queries
⇨ To improve data quality

Data warehousing and data mining

If the introduction of these systems is to provide competitive advantage to the firm there are a number of management issues which must be addressed and these can be categorised as data management, process management and security management

Data management

There is an ISO standard which addresses the rules, principals and guidelines for classification, attribution, definition, naming, standardisation and registration of data elements to ensure consistent quality of meta data. Meta data has been described as the most appropriate tool for quality assurance in this context

Process management

This will be an iterative process since the business environment and the firm itself are constantly changing and the data warehouse should be subject to continuous improvement

Security management

A data warehouse will need special security not only because of the value of the data contained therein but because of the risks of contamination if there is unauthorised dumping of data into the system

Regarding data warehousing and mining

You should make sure that you are aware of the advantages and disadvantages of this topic – you could be asked to justify the introduction of such a system and also to explain how it should be implemented

Strategic Implications of IT

This chapter will examine the different ways in which the information system might lead the organisation towards competitive advantage by taking a strategic approach to information technology

Topics

- The strategic case for IT investment
- Using IT to gain competitive advantage
- Using information for competitive advantage
- Value-added networks
- Using e-commerce for competitive advantage
- The need for information systems strategies
- The changing role of the IT department
- Organisational knowledge management
- Developing a knowledge strategy

Key learning system questions

5.2 IT strategy
5.3 Outsourcing
5.4 Knowledge strategy

The strategic case for IT investment

Within an organisation there is normally a need to have three different strategies relating to the information being used:

⇨ Information technology
⇨ Information systems
⇨ Information management

There are long lists detailing why an information technology strategy is necessary. Principal amongst these is the high cost of the equipment, the potential for competitive advantage if done properly and the downside risks if the strategy is wrong. The justification will be different for different types of organisation

Three strategies are defined as:

'Information technology strategy refers to the hardware configuration that an organisation requires to transfer information. Information systems strategy relates to the long-term plan concerned with the use of IT within the organisation. Information management strategy refers to the approach to managing data and information within the organisation, specifically how data and information are stored and accessed'

Information technology strategy

You should make sure that you are aware of all of the reasons that can be used to justify IT strategy and be able to relate them to specific organisation types in scenarios

The strategic case for IT investment

Information systems and information management strategies

The information systems strategy is normally decided first, immediately after the firm has decided its long-term goals. Once the systems strategy is decided, the information technology strategy can be decided defining which physical systems are in place. Finally, the information management strategy can be determined to specify how the organisation will deal with and store the information gathered. Nolan has suggested a model for the evolution of information systems which, although dated, is still relevant

Regarding information systems evolution

You may be presented, in a scenario, with a situation where the organisation appears to be in one stage of evolution, whilst the management approach being adopted is more appropriate to a different stage. You need to be able to recognise this and make justified recommendations as to how the appropriate changes might be brought about

The strategic case for IT investment

The applications portfolio

The importance of IT to an organisation has been
described by means of a 2×2 matrix plotting the strategic
importance of current information systems versus the
strategic importance of planned information systems.
The matrix classifies organisations into four types:

⇨ Strategic – the firm depends upon the information
system for it's competitive advantage
⇨ Turnaround – the business expects that the
information will become strategically important in the
future
⇨ Support – the firm can currently see no strategic
value in it's information system
⇨ Factory – the business sees the strategic importance
of its information systems now, but expects this to
diminish in the future

It would seem unlikely that any modern firm would
classify itself in the 'factory' box of the matrix

An alternative classification gives the following:

⇨ Support – application improve management
effectiveness but are not critical. Typically
accounting systems, spreadsheets, payroll systems
and legally required systems
⇨ Key operational – critical to sustaining the business.
Typically inventory control, production control and
order management
⇨ Strategic – critical to future business success
⇨ High potential – innovative and have promise.
Typically expert systems and the Internet

Using IT to gain competitive advantage

Competitive advantage

'Using knowledge of the competitive forces to put the organisation in a position where it exerts more competitive force on others than they do on it'

Porter said that competitive advantage can only be achieved by:

⇨ Low cost – the lowest production costs in the industry or

⇨ Differentiation – persuading customers that the product is better, different or unique in some way

He subsequently said that there are three ways where the information revolution affects competition:

⇨ IT changes the industry structure and, hence, the rules of competition

⇨ IT creates competitive advantage by giving companies new ways to outperform their rivals

⇨ It spawns new businesses, often from within a company's existing operations

He further suggested that the value chain (both the activities and the linkages) could be used to give an indication of the strategic potential of the information system since:

'Every value activity has both a physical component and an information processing component. The latter encompasses the steps required to capture, manipulate and channel the data necessary to perform the activity.'

Using IT to gain competitive advantage

The proposed agenda for exploiting the information system is:

1. Assess the information intensity of the industry
2. Determine the role of information technology in the industry structure
3. Identify and rank the ways in which IT might create a competitive advantage
4. Investigate how IT might engender new businesses
5. Develop a plan for taking advantage of IT

Gaining competitive advantage using IT

From your broader reading, you should think of examples of companies that have used IT to give themselves a low cost advantage or a differentiation advantage. Dell might be one example, Amazon, another

Using information for competitive advantage

It is possible to classify industries according to their information characteristics both in terms of the number of information exchanges necessary and the extent to which information is a component of the product. For instance the information content of cement is very low but for consulting is very high. In terms of the number of information exchanges this is high in airlines but low in the fashion industry

Gaining competitive advantage using information

From your broader reading, you should think of examples of companies that have used information to give themselves a low cost advantage or a differentiation advantage. Whilst you do this remember that it is not just the activities in the value chain that are important, but also the linkages between them as well. You should also consider the linkages between the value chains of different companies

Value-added networks

'A network to which services have been added, normally by a third party, over and above the basic ability to transfer data'

VAN's will directly add value to an organisations products or services and tend to arise from collaborative ventures between organisations with a common interest. The users are often within the same value system (you might want to look back to earlier comments about the value net). VAN's usually differ from other communications networks in that they are usually external to the organisation and are shared and paid for. Since organisations will look for a sustainable competitive advantage it is worth remembering that once everyone in the industry joins a VAN, it will no longer provide competitive advantage but will become a threshold skill

Using e-commerce for competitive advantage

E-commerce

'The use of electronic techniques, including the Internet, to sell products and services'

E-marketing, by contrast, is usually used to describe the promotion of products using the Internet

Establishing an e-commerce strategy

The usual stages in setting up a particular strategy would need to be incorporated but particular points of note are:

⇨ Is e-commerce compatible with what the firm does?
⇨ Will there be an adverse effect on other aspects of the business? For example, will e-commerce create new sales or just take them away from the traditional business?
⇨ A full cost benefit analysis will need to be conducted – writing and maintaining web sites is an expensive operation
⇨ Will the web site be written in-house or outsourced?
⇨ Will the maintenance be in-house or outsourced?

Impact of e-commerce and the Internet

If an Internet site is established it's impact upon the business may be quite pronounced. Through your broader reading you give some thought to the changes in the firms operations that are likely to occur because they have taken this step

The need for information systems strategies

Many organisations now realise that their information system has the potential to be a strategic resource and, as such should have a formal strategy. This should bring about the following benefits:

⇨ Achieving goal congruence between corporate objectives and information systems objectives
⇨ Greater likelihood of achieving and sustaining competitive advantage
⇨ Better focus of the high level of expenditure necessary
⇨ Timely exploitation of IT developments (not always when they are first available)

The information system should have a separate, but linked, strategy because:

⇨ It is an adaptive, open system
⇨ The organisation exists in a dynamic environment and information needs are constantly changing

⇨ The organisation relies upon the information system to construct it's strategic plan

Regarding information systems strategies

You should spend some time refreshing your memory on the typical contents of IS, IT and IM strategies and how they should be developed. Whilst doing this do not forget the importance of collaborative strategies that have recently been gaining importance

The changing role of the IT department

Looking back to Nolan's model that we mentioned at the beginning of this chapter, the first four stages are relevant in describing how IT departments have changed. At the integration stage of Nolan's model we start to see genuine communication between the IT department and the functions of the firm. The organisation of the MIS department can take a number of forms depending on the functional and physical organisation of the firm. In many organisations, there will be some form of matrix structure. Alternatives are:

⇨ Star organisation – typically found in retail chains
⇨ Partially distributed organisation – remote geographical locations performing different, but related, tasks
⇨ Fully distributed organisation – a virtual organisation

Downsizing the IT function

As organisations increasingly tried to focus on those core activities where competitive advantage could be developed, they started to outsource various service functions. IT was no exception. There are certain risks associated with downsizing IT departments:

⇨ The organisation might lose the ability to maintain or develop major systems that might be of strategic benefit
⇨ The organisation will lose the knowledge of key staff, and may be unable to repair or modify existing systems
⇨ The controls over the information system may be relaxed, leading to increased error and failure rates
⇨ The organisation may have to incur significant costs to replace staff with external consultants in time of crisis

The changing role of the IT department

With this in mind, careful planning is necessary and the optimum level of support must be determined. This has led to the development of 'information centres' with the key functions of:

⇨ A help desk function to assist users possibly involving remote diagnostic software

⇨ Advice on application development – this is essential where an organisation allows staff to write their own applications. This approach can help to ensure that the firm's standards are maintained

⇨ Purchasing standards and testing of potential acquisitions of software can be enforced

⇨ Network traffic can be monitored and upgrades proposed when necessary

⇨ Prototype development can be conducted

⇨ Data management, including the management of corporate databases or a data warehouse

Outsourcing IT

Outsourcing generally is a very current topic at the moment and you should be aware of the issues from your broader reading. You will be familiar with the arguments for and against the approach from your studies at the *Organisational Management and Information Systems*. It would be a good idea to revise those arguments since this topic is examinable for this paper

Organisational knowledge management

A relatively new area, this is one of the fastest growing areas of management consultancy

Knowledge workers

'Those who have high levels of education and specialist skills, combined with the ability to apply those skills to identify and solve problems'

There is a link between knowledge management and the concept of the learning organisation but in the mid-1990s, the two topics diverged. Whereas the learning organisation has the following characteristics:

⇨ Broad focus
⇨ Theory driven
⇨ 'Building' metaphor
⇨ Systems-based view of the firm

⇨ Emphasis on cultural management
⇨ Emphasis on managing tacit knowledge
⇨ Responsibility of strategic/HR managers

The contrasting focus for knowledge management is:

⇨ Specific focus
⇨ Practice driven
⇨ 'Mining' metaphor
⇨ Resource-based view of the firm
⇨ Emphasis of IS management
⇨ Emphasis on changing tacit knowledge into explicit knowledge
⇨ Responsibility of IS managers or Chief Knowledge Officers

Organisational knowledge management

Knowledge

'A fluid mix of framed experience, values, contextual information and expert insight that provides a framework for evaluating and incorporating new experiences and information. It originates in the minds of knowers. In organisations, it often becomes embedded not only in documents or repositories but also in organisational routines, practices, processes and norms'

The following categorisation of knowledge is useful:

⇨ Know what – the knowledge of facts
⇨ Know how – the knowledge of processes
⇨ Know why – the recognition of how the process fits with others
⇨ Care why – the development of values to support the process

The main objective of knowledge management is to capture all of the first three of these and make them available as a resource to everyone in the organisation. The fourth is more the concern of the learning organisation

Knowledge can be acquired by individuals in the following ways:

⇨ From the education process
⇨ From the experience of performing tasks
⇨ From the observation of others
⇨ From formal knowledge exchange (training and coaching)
⇨ From informal knowledge exchange (brainstorming/meetings/anecdotes)

Organisational knowledge management

Information is turned into knowledge by:

⇨ Comparison – how does this situation compare with other, known, situations?

⇨ Consequences – what implications does this information have?

⇨ Connections – how does this information relate to other bits of information?

⇨ Conversation – what do other people think about this information?

You should note that all of these are questions and arranging an atmosphere where an enquiring mind is encouraged is good for knowledge transfer!

Developing a knowledge strategy

There are five main steps in the development and implementation of a knowledge strategy:

1. Getting senior management support
2. Creating the appropriate technological infrastructure
3. Creating the appropriate database structures
4. Creating a 'sharing' culture – often the most difficult stage. Most people believe that 'knowledge is power' and are often loathe to give theirs away!
5. Populating the databases and using the knowledge

Information technology infrastructure

The organisational management system provided by the company to help knowledge workers can vary from the most simple (e-mail to share and databases to store knowledge) to the more complicated involving Intranets, online access to specific Intranet sites and data mining tools. This will help with the gathering and sharing of explicit knowledge but tacit knowledge, which exists in the brains of the employees, will need to be surfaced by other means. In some cases they may not be aware of its existence – it is used instinctively rather than deliberately

Knowledge sharing systems

There are a number of systems available to facilitate knowledge sharing. They include:

⇨ Groupware – range of tools designed to assist communication, a well-known example is Lotus Notes. Tools will include discussion databases, shared diaries, task lists, diary pages, address book and some form of reminder system – electronic post – it notes
⇨ Workflow – will route projects through a set of tasks and employees so that the work is completed in the optimum fashion

Developing a knowledge strategy

⇨ Intranets – an information sharing system built on Internet technology
⇨ Extranet – similar to an Intranet but access is allowed to third parties outside the organisation. Becoming increasingly popular as a source of competitive advantage particularly when used with diagnostic software for the remote maintenance of the customer's equipment

Cultural issues

Human nature is the biggest barrier to knowledge management as we have mentioned and 'knowledge hoarding' is more common than 'knowledge sharing.' Knowledge sharing can be encouraged by:

⇨ Lead from the front – a clear and obvious commitment is important

⇨ Invest time and money – not just in the infrastructure but in the people and specific appointments
⇨ Reward knowledge sharing – make it part of the appraisal process
⇨ Hire knowledge sharers – make it part person specification when hiring

The benefits of organisational knowledge management

The following benefits are claimed:

⇨ Higher workforce motivation levels and reduction in unproductive time
⇨ Greater corporate coherence – everyone has a clearer understanding of objectives and values

Developing a knowledge strategy

⇨ A richer 'knowledge stock' leading to an increased ability to compete and add value

⇨ A stronger 'meritocracy of ideas' where staffs are encouraged to generate and use knowledge to innovate

Regarding knowledge management

Since knowledge management is one of the latest 'new things,' you should have gathered quite a lot of information from your broader reading. That, together with what you learnt about organisational learning in an earlier paper should equip you to answer questions on the advantages and disadvantages of knowledge management systems, and the steps a firm should go through to install such a system and to encourage its success

Strategic Options and their Evaluation

This chapter will consider the directions in which the management may choose to take the firm and how they should evaluate those choices

Topics

- Three sets of strategic choices
- Porter's generic competitive strategy model
- Product–market strategies
- Alternative growth strategies
- International growth strategies
- Resource-based view of strategy

- Divestment strategies
- Strategic options in the public sector
- Strategic options in the charity sector
- Evaluation of options

Key learning system questions

6.1 Overseas expansion
6.4 Acquisitions
6.5 Product–market strategies

Development strategies

Having done all of the analysis that we have covered in the previous chapters, the management of a firm is faced with three fundamental choices:

1. The basis of choice – dependent upon the corporate purpose and aspirations
2. The choice of direction – will the firm decide to protect and build, penetrate the market, develop new products, develop new markets or diversify? Or possibly a combination of these?
3. The choice of method – will they decide to do this by internal development, merger and acquisition, or joint venture and alliances?

Porter's generic competitive strategy model

As we have discussed before, Porter claimed that to be successful, the management of a firm must chose to adopt (only) one of the following approaches:

⇨ Overall cost leadership
⇨ Differentiation
⇨ Focus

To try to do more than one of these would lead to dilution of effort and sub-optimal performance. The model was developed from Porters work on competitive forces, which we have discussed previously

Using Porter's model

It is claimed that the model can be used to help management to arrange and classify their thoughts

1. To help analyse the competitive position of rivals – to spot gaps in the industry and to help avoid head-on collision

2. To analyse the risks of the present strategy
3. To help decide the appropriate competitive strategy for the firm

Limitations of Porter's model

Porter's model has been in use for over 20 years and is still very popular. However, there are limitations some of which have arisen as the business world has changed

⇨ There is a lack of clarity in the definition of 'industry' – increasingly this has become a problem as boundaries have blurred
⇨ The strategic unit is ill defined – although Porter talks about firms, often these are divisions of larger entities and it is difficult to consider them separately
⇨ Evidence shows that there are a number of firms who do mix their strategic approaches and still

make healthy profits. The consumer is often happy with acceptable levels of product performance rather than extreme low cost or extreme differentiation

⇨ The model is prescriptive and, in general, prescriptions do not work all of the time – if only because the firm's rivals are just as aware of the prescriptions!

⇨ Theoretically it restricts the firm to its present industry – it doesn't cater for those firms who would attempt to expand the industry or even move to another

Regarding Porter's generic strategies

Despite the criticisms of Porter's model, it is important that you are aware of the prescriptions made within it and how they tie into the five forces model that we discussed earlier. Remember that, together, they give a framework for management to structure the analysis of an industry and the strategies of rivals and themselves. As such, it could be a useful way for you to structure a similar analysis in an examination question

The Ansoff matrix

Another model that demonstrates the four generic approaches open to management:

⇨ Market penetration – same products in same markets. Here the company intends to persuade the existing customers to buy more of the same product – usually by modifying the marketing mix (which we discussed earlier)

⇨ Market development strategy – same products in new markets. The company will find new markets or modify (usually by segmentation) the existing market

⇨ Product development strategy – modified products in existing markets. Changes are made to the product so that customers will want to buy and consume more

⇨ Diversification strategies – doing something different. This can be done either by related diversification where either the product technology or the marketing methods are the same – but not both. This is sometimes known as concentric diversification. Alternatively, the firm can attempt unrelated diversification – neither the product technology nor the marketing methods are related. This is sometimes known as conglomerate diversification

As we have gone down this list, the risk has increased. We can consider Coca Cola as a practical example

⇨ Market penetration – the largest market for Cola is the teenager market and it is sold on street credibility – heavy advertising by pop stars is used to increase market penetration

⇨ Market development – segmenting the market by different package sizes to appeal to families, economy and bulk buyers

Product development – product modifications such as taking out the sugar or the caffeine may convince the existing market to buy more

⇨ Diversification – both Coca Cola and Pepsico have invested in other products, for instance, Coca Cola owns a snack company called Frito Lay

As with Porter's model you will often find that the strategy adopted by a firm appears to be a hybrid of the above classifications

Strategic development and risk

As noted above risk increases as the company moves further away from purely market penetration and become particularly acute when diversification is contemplated. Risk can be considered as:

⇨ Market risk – new markets with existing players, or brand new markets which are completely unknown

⇨ Product risk – development of new products carries not only the risk of not succeeding but the overall

⇨ Operational and management risk – whilst attempting new ventures the management which they may not be good at, may also lose their grip on the existing business

⇨ Financial risk – shareholders are inherently conservative and any 'new venture' may cause them unease

Regarding directional strategies

You should make sure that you are aware of the concept of generic strategies, be able to discuss their limitations and the risks involved in each suggested strategy. You should also be able to recommend which strategy a company should adopt in a 'real' situation. Your broader reading should help you by letting you see what real companies have done in real situations

Alternative growth strategies

Internal development

This involves the firm in using it's own resources to develop products and services, staff and markets and is also known as organic growth. To be successful, the company will need to be good at the management of innovation. The inspiration for innovation can come from either market pull – the customers let you know they want something new, or from technology push – you have developed something and look for markets in which to exploit it. Not all technological innovation leads to new products since it can come in the form of product innovation – where the customer sees something new, or process innovation where the firm develops a better, more efficient way of manufacturing a product. In this case the firm may enjoy considerable cost advantage but the customer will not 'see' a new product. This is claimed to be a negative correlation between expenditure on research and development and profitability, and many successful companies obtain their new product knowledge via strategic alliances rather than purely by in house development

Regarding internal development

You should make sure that you are aware of the advantages and disadvantages of both internal development and the acquisition of new technology via alliances. It would also be a good idea to be able to discuss what management can do to foster an innovative culture in an organisation

Joint development strategies

Earlier, we discussed the situation where firms cooperate with buyers (or suppliers) to jointly exploit an opportunity or market. This can be done with varying degrees of formality. Remember that cartels are illegal and organisations like the European Union (which we discussed earlier) are likely to fine cartel members heavily

The form of legal cooperative ventures can be:

⇨ **Joint venture**. The partners, who may be from different businesses, form a separate company in which each hold an equity stake. The possible advantages are: the reduction of risk to capital, the access to partners competences, don't end up competing with each other, may permit entry to partners host market. The potential disadvantages are: poorly written heads of agreement may lead to disputes, loss of confidential information, disputes about allocation of costs and effort and lack of support from parent groups

⇨ **Strategic alliances**. A group of companies, often from the same industry, agree to work together to exploit a common advantage. There are varying degrees of formality and it may only be an agreement to cooperate or something more solid like a swapping of equity. The advantages are broadly the same as those for a joint venture but the additional disadvantages are that they are more likely to attract the attention of the competition authorities and, to the outside world they may look disjointed and unconvincing

⇨ **Franchises**. A firm will decide to expand its business by granting other, usually smaller, firms the right to use its business systems and reputational capital. (Think of McDonald's and Body Shop.) The advantages to the franchiser are: rapid expansion using someone else's capital investment, reduced cost of control, minimised investment in non-core activities, dynamism of local management and control over franchisee to the extent of the agreement. The disadvantages are that: there are reduced profits, there is a need to monitor franchisees, the reputation of the brand is in the hands of others who may leave and become rivals

⇨ **Licences**. Similar to a franchise but there is less central control and less, or even no, support from the licensor

Regarding joint development

You should make sure that you are aware of the advantages and disadvantages of each approach and when each would be most appropriate for a firm to employ. From your broader reading, try to identify examples of each of the approaches and justify, for yourself, the decision that the firms have made when choosing that development route. Try to link these approaches back to Porter's five forces model to see where competitive advantage is being gained

Mergers and acquisitions

This involves the combination of two, originally separate, firms. Technically there is a difference between mergers and acquisitions and you will have learnt about those differences elsewhere, together with the various methods used to value target companies

It has been suggested that the main beneficiaries of acquisitions are the management of the acquiring firm and that their motivation is:

⇨ To pursue growth in the size of the firm – increase their status

⇨ For self-actualisation – making use of their talents and skills

⇨ For self-preservation – increased job security by diversify risk

⇨ For self-preservation – reducing the risk of takeover

There is, however, a business case for acquisitions and these are the following advantages:

⇨ Firm acquires the expertise and contacts of the target firm

⇨ Firm eliminates a potential rival in the market

⇨ Firm gains swifter entry to the market than by internal development

⇨ Firm may spread some risk if the target is somewhat diversified

⇨ Firm enjoys lower commercial risk since target is established in the market

⇨ Firm may get a 'bargain' if the target is undervalued by investors or the current management is under performing

There are however, some drawbacks:

⇨ It is difficult to arrive at an accurate valuation even in a 'friendly' takeover

Alternative growth strategies

⇨ There is a high cost of post acquisition integration of systems both financially, operationally and emotionally

⇨ There is a need for rationalisation to be rapid and may distract management from running the original business

⇨ There may be morale problems in the acquired company and, if it is a service company, their leaving will cause further problems since they are the assets

⇨ Very high initial capital costs

⇨ If done too often, it may damage firm's reputation with it's own shareholders

⇨ Failure to win a bid can also damage reputation

Value creation logic

Whilst a firm is looking for acquisition targets, there should be a clear set of criteria applied to the search, screening, identification and evaluation of potential targets. An essential part of this is the value creation logic. This can be summarised as follows:

⇨ The target is undervalued in the stock market – share price does not represent earnings potential

⇨ The predator's management could do a better job than the present management

⇨ There are potential synergies between the acquiring and target companies

⇨ The acquisition will protect the firm from potential hostile competition that would arise if another company were to acquire the target

⇨ The target has assets which can be sold off without harming the performance – asset stripping

Regarding mergers and acquisitions

You should be aware of the advantages and disadvantages of mergers and acquisitions and how they are valued. It is also important that you should be able to discuss the stages in the acquisition process. Please remember that post acquisition management is often difficult and many of the problems are cultural, it would help you to look back to the work you did in *Integrated Management* to make sure you could discuss these issues fully

Types of international growth

In addition to the methods of growth discussed so far, companies can expand outside their home countries by:

⇨ Exporting, having manufactured in the home base
⇨ Manufacture in the target market
⇨ Operate as a multinational – here there is a deliberate policy of coordinating value, adding activities across national boundaries and internalising cross-border trades
⇨ Operate as a global corporation – a truly 'nationless' organisation where there is no apparent, or obvious, home country
⇨ Use a contract manufacturing service in the target market

With all of these approaches and the ones discussed earlier there are some issues which management must consider:

⇨ Social responsibility – considerations such as: pay and conditions under different labour laws, health and safety legislation, political or social exclusion of particular ethnic groups, bribery and other forms of corruption
⇨ Development effects on the local economy – considerations of technology transfer, training of local staff and involvement in infrastructure building
⇨ Cross-cultural management – considerations of language differences, customs and social mores, attitude to management and desire for participation
⇨ Financial control of operations – considerations of foreign exchange and currency translation, transfer price legislation and repatriation rules

Regarding international growth strategies

Many of the considerations regarding international growth are the same as those for any other growth strategy however, there are particular issues for companies intending to expand abroad. You should make sure that you are aware of these and use them in any evaluation of a decision that you are required to make on behalf of a company. This will be particularly important in terms of the risks involved

Resource-based view of strategy

So far, we have been discussing the positioning approach to strategic management. You will be familiar with the resource-based view of strategy from your studies at *P5 Integrated Management*. To refresh your memory the resources that are considered to give a firm competitive advantage are:

⇨ Assets – if rare and important they qualify as strategic assets

⇨ Capabilities – things the firm has learnt to do with its assets

⇨ Competences – deeper seated capabilities, routines that have developed over time from bundles of capabilities

To qualify as strategic resources, need to be: rare, valuable, difficult to acquire, copy or imitate

Comments on resource-based view of strategy

There are a number of issues:

1. There is a conflict with conventional product/market-based views of strategy
2. It is difficult to cope with a dynamic environment under this view
3. The view challenges the rational model of strategy
4. RBT can lead to different conclusions to the more conventional approach
5. There is a very little empirical evidence to support RBT

Regarding the resource-based view of strategy

You should be able to compare and contrast the positioning view with the resource-based view of strategy. You have only been given an overview of RBT here and you are strongly recommended to go back to your notes for *P5 Integrated Management* to flesh these out

Divestment strategies

There are a variety of reasons why a firm may chose to withdraw from a particular product/market combination:

1. To liquidate assets in the business unit to remove a loss making subsidiary
2. To present a more coherent investment to the shareholders and other funders
3. To facilitate better control
4. To avoid takeovers by removing value gaps
5. To enable management to focus on core competences
6. To realise cash for other purposes
7. To provide an exit route for investors

There are a number of methods by which a company may choose to divest a subsidiary or component of the business

⇨ Sale as a going concern to another business
⇨ Closure and liquidation of the assets
⇨ Sale by management by out (MBO) or management by in (MBI)
⇨ Demerger – if the parent group maintains a majority shareholding in the new company this is often referred to as an equity carve out

Each of these approaches has merits and demerits, and much will depend upon the motivation of the divesting company

Regarding divestment

Use your broader reading to identify examples of companies that have divested themselves of part of their business by each of these methods. What advantage did they achieve by doing it in the way they did? Was there a better way that they could have achieved the same result? Don't only think of the 'hard' factors in your answer to these questions but consider the 'softer' issues of management as well

Strategic options in the public sector

'Strategic management in the public sector, is concerned with strengthening the long-term health and effectiveness of governmental units and leading them through positive change to ensure a continuing productive fit with their environments.' This might not sound very different to the strategic management of a commercial organisation but there are few fundamental differences

⇨ Quite often the public sector is only judged on the ability to stay within budget

⇨ Since governments are subject to regular elections, the objectives may change and the long-term is, by definition, shorter

⇨ Although some governments talk of customers or clients those that pay for the services are often different from those that receive them – the beneficiaries

⇨ There are invariably a larger and more diverse group of stakeholders whose interests and values must be considered

⇨ There are often conflicting objectives to be met and the public sector will often have to satisfice those objectives rather than take the optimal decision

Regarding the public sector

Whilst many of the analysis methods we have discussed cannot be used with the public sector, there is a place for the value chain and you should make sure that you are able to translate its use to this environment. Arguably, the most important consideration is to ensure that any decision making process, yours for a question, or the one you propose for a government department takes the requirements of the various stakeholders into account and is rigorous in its evaluations

Strategic options in the charity sector

As with the public sector, there is a little place for the prescriptive models described earlier but a number of the analysis models can be used or adapted when dealing with charities

The options available to charities have been described as:

⇨ Putting in place the value chain, structure and systems that allow the NPO's mission to be implemented

⇨ Develop a fundraising structure that allows income to be generated, in quantity, and in the most regular, predictable and reliable forms available

⇨ Providing visible evidence that management of the NPO is being carried out in a transparent, professional and competent manner

Regarding the charity sector

Most authors agree that the most important, and difficult, thing for a charity to do is an analysis of stakeholders. In any question involving a charity, it is likely to be very important for you as well

Evaluation of options

Any option that an organisation is contemplating can be evaluated under the following three criteria:

⇨ Suitability test – is this the correct choice given the circumstances in which the firm finds itself?
⇨ Acceptability test – will this option gain the support and acceptance of those stakeholders who are important and powerful?
⇨ Feasibility test – is this something that the firm is capable of achieving at the required level of success?
⇨ Sustainability test – if we adopt this option, will it contribute to the firm's long-term competitive advantage? With the pressure on short-term results most options do not do well against this criteria but, bearing in mind how difficult it is to achieve sustainable competitive advantage – that is not really surprising

The majority of strategic decisions that a firm has to make will not be clear cut and will usually have considerable uncertainty built into them. The quality of the assumptions made will be very important as in a number of cases there will be a need for a 'judgement call' by senior management

Regarding the evaluation of options

From *P5 Integrated Management* you will be aware of the differences between decisions at the strategic, tactical and operational level. If you are given a free hand in a question to suggest options for a firm rather than evaluate options which have been presented to you, try to make sure that your proposals are strategic rather than tactical. You will be aware of the investment appraisal, management accounting and financial management techniques which are available for the quantitative analysis of options you will certainly need to use them. However, you should make sure, you are able to discuss the merits of an option on non-financial basis – this is not an exact science!

Organisational Impacts of Business Strategy

This chapter will consider the implications of strategic change on the organisation

Key learning system questions

7.1 Business process
    re-engineering

7.2 Public sector management

Topics

- Leading issues in business organisation
- Contemporary approaches to organisation
- Business process re-engineering
- New patterns of employment
- Implications for management accounting
- Strategic change

Organisations

'Organisations are social arrangements for achieving controlled performance of collective goals'

It is important to note from this definition that 'arrangements' can mean structure, the assets controlled, rules and processes, levels of authority and their operation and relationships with other 'arrangements.' 'Social' implies the importance of people in these arrangements and so motivation, culture, political behaviour and the need to modify and control behaviour are important. The 'controls' mentioned will need to be changed if the purpose and strategic intent of the organisation is changed. This will have implications for management accountants since they will need to provide the mechanics of control. As the strategy changes, there may be a need for the control techniques to change with

them – the management accountant will need to be aware of the appropriate techniques and how the change process can be managed – this means you!

Organisational structures

You will have learnt at *P5 Integrated Management* to distinguish between, and describe the advantages and disadvantages of, the following structures:

⇨ Simple organisation
⇨ Functional organisation
⇨ Multidimensional organisation
⇨ Holding company structure
⇨ Matrix organisation structure

You should make sure that you still understand these, as well as the classical school of management as described by Fayol and the contingency theory approach described by Lynch

Contemporary approaches to organisation

The need for alternatives to the classical model of the organisation has arisen because of:

⇨ The breakdown of long-term planning due to the increased complexity and dynamism
⇨ The popularity of the resource-based school of strategic management
⇨ The increased power of stakeholder groups outside the organisation
⇨ The greater need for innovation in product and processes
⇨ The advent of the information age and the greater need for information from outside the organisation
⇨ The greater need for organisational flexibility

Competition in the third wave

The 'third wave' will create an information society and this will have pronounced implications for organisations:

⇨ The importance of the service sector will continue to increase
⇨ The form of trading relationships will change as network relationships emerge
⇨ Consumer tastes will globalise and so will organisations
⇨ The importance of knowledge workers will increase

Kanter

At this point you should read your notes from *P5 Integrated Management* on the work of R. M. Kanter

This will lead to the following management issues:

⇨ Strategy – pursue renewal not retrenchment
⇨ Customer value – match competences to customers
⇨ Knowledge management – leverage knowledge for competitive advantage
⇨ Business organisation – organise around networks and processes
⇨ Market focus – find and keep strategic, profitable and loyal customers
⇨ Management accounting – manage the business, not the numbers
⇨ Measurement and control – strike a new balance between control and empowerment
⇨ Shareholder value – measure intellectual assets
⇨ Productivity – encourage and reward value creating work
⇨ Transformation – adapt the third wave model

Another recent approach talks of the impact of chaos theory and complex adaptive systems (which we referred to earlier) on management and Stacey talks of 'Extraordinary management' and suggests the following intervention steps for management:

⇨ Develop new perspectives on control
⇨ Design the use of power
⇨ Establish self-organising groups
⇨ Develop multiple cultures
⇨ Improve group learning skills
⇨ Present challenges and take risks
⇨ Create resource slack

Regarding recent management theories

All of these thoughts together with what you learned at *P5 Integrated Management* imply that there are changes which will have to be accommodated by management accountants in the organisation of the future. You should read Section 7.3.6. Future developments in management practice in the manual and make sure that you can make recommendations to management as to how these changes can be managed. It is particularly important that, you look back to what we said about network organisations and be able to answer the questions posed in the manual under Section 7.4.1

Business process re-engineering

'The selection of areas of business activity in which repeatable and repeated sets of activities are undertaken, and the development of improved understanding of how they operate and of the scope for radical redesign with a view to creating and delivering better customer value'

Principles of re-engineering

Hammer proposed seven principles of re-engineering:

1. Organise around outcomes not tasks
2. Have those who use the output of the process to perform the process
3. Subsume information processing work into the real work that produces the information
4. Treat geographically – dispersed resources as though they were centralised
5. Link parallel activities instead of integrating tasks
6. Put the decision point where the work is performed and build control into the process
7. Capture information once, and at the source

Stages in a BPR process

These are recognised to be five stages:

⇨ Identify the process for innovation
⇨ Identify the change levers
⇨ Develop the process vision
⇨ Understand the existing process
⇨ Design and prototype the new process

Thoughts on BPR

It is argued that BPR is predominantly intended to increase the firms ability to deliver value to the customer. This will, therefore be one of the features of an investment appraisal exercise evaluating BPR. However, the argument that processes will be streamlined cannot be ignored and should also be factored into the calculation

It is argued that BPR:

⇨ Draws on Porter's value chain by considering the firm as set of value creating activities
⇨ Can support the marketing orientation of the firm
⇨ Can be assisted by benchmarking
⇨ Can be used to further the network organisation
⇨ Can bring into focus the relationship between the firm and its suppliers

⇨ However, it is often seen as the pretext for staff reductions
⇨ It conflicts with human resource-based approaches to business improvement
⇨ Overlooks the impact of human resources
⇨ Can increase stress on staff
⇨ Focuses on business efficiency not business effectiveness
⇨ May destroy the basis for existing controls within the organisation

New patterns of employment

You should, at this stage, refer back to your notes for *P5 Integrated Management* and make sure that you understand the concepts of flexible firms and virtual organisations

The changes for methods of managing organisations can be summarised as:

⇨ The need for greater use of teams
⇨ Increase empowerment and delegation to lower levels
⇨ Creation of new 'network' relations across the value net
⇨ Increased importance for the knowledge worker
⇨ Need for new systems of management information and control

The implications for management accounting are:

⇨ Potential breakdown in management control
⇨ Need for additional performance measurement systems
⇨ Greater participation in the management decision process
⇨ Revision of budgetary control systems
⇨ Changes to the employment patterns for management accountants themselves

There are further implications for management accounting systems, these are:

1. Increased empowerment and accountability leading to:
    ⇨ Need to control opportunism
    ⇨ New forms of control
    ⇨ Increased use of electronic information systems
    ⇨ Information must be directed to the shop floor as well
    ⇨ A need to define new responsibility centres that criss – cross functions
    ⇨ Decisions to identify the boundaries of teams so that each can become a measurable unit

New patterns of employment

2. Motivation and remuneration
3. Managing the business not the numbers
   ⇨ Switch from vertical reporting to horizontal reporting
   ⇨ Switch from cost control to developing cost reduction processes
   ⇨ Strike a new balance between empowerment and control

Regarding flexibility and new structures

There is a lot to assimilate here and there is a very strong need to use your notes from *P5 Integrated Management*

Please remember this discussion, when we come to talk about the balanced scorecard in the next chapter

You will have already considered change and change management for *Organisational Management and Information Systems* – please refresh your memory. We can categorise change under three headings:

⇨ Incremental change – quite common
⇨ Major change – rarer, usually caused by a significant decline in performance
⇨ Transformational change – very rare, made necessary by sharp, deep decline and imminent failure of an organisation

Planning change

As with the expression 'failing to plan is planning to fail,' we can say the same about planning change. Rehearsal is essential. The stage are as follows:

⇨ Assess the extent of the proposed change
⇨ Analyse the potential stakeholder reactions
⇨ Assess the stakeholders power and influence
⇨ Identify ways to overcome that resistance
⇨ Enact the change process

Overcoming resistance

For resistance to be overcome there needs to be some element of power available:

⇨ Power of resources
⇨ Power of processes
⇨ Power of meaning

Strategic change

Resistance is more likely to be overcome and change successful if:

⇨ There are clear understandable goals
⇨ There are realistic timeframes
⇨ There is clear guidance regarding acceptable individual behaviours
⇨ There is clear unified leadership
⇨ Decentralisation and empowerment precede integration and control
⇨ There is sufficient investment in training

There is no recipe for success, each situation is different!

Regarding strategic change

Much of this will be familiar to you from your earlier studies but the relevance of this material for this paper cannot be stressed too much. Since many of the questions you could be asked involve strategic decisions and their subsequent implementation – change is an essential component of your study

Implementing and Controlling Plans

This chapter will consider how an organisation can make things happen
and ensure that it stays on track

Key learning system questions

8.1 Management accounting in the public sector

8.4 Performance measurement

8.5 Divisional performance

8.6 Balanced scorecard

Topics

- Theories of control
- Profit-related measures and value-based methods
- The role of the corporate centre
- Management accounting and performance management
- Multidimensional performance measurement
- Stakeholder measures
- Multinational industries

Theories of control

You are strongly recommended to review your work for *Management Accounting – Performance Evaluation* and for *Organisational Management and Information Systems.* Control is often thought of as being 'a process of ensuring that which was supposed to happen actually happens.' For management control to be effective it must

⇨ Regulate the process of formulating purpose and
⇨ Regulate the process of purpose achievement

Hopwood identified three forms of control in organisations:

⇨ Administrative control
⇨ Social controls
⇨ Self-control

Although we are primarily interested in performance measurement, it is best if these do not clash with the other forms of control in the organisation. The functions of performance measurement can be defined as:

⇨ Check position
⇨ Communicate position
⇨ Confirm priorities
⇨ Compel progress

Profit-related measures and value-based methods

Regarding the measures used

At this point you should revisit your earlier studies and ensure that you are completely familiar with the advantages and disadvantages, and calculation of profit-related measures

Opportunity cost of capital-based measures

Shareholder wealth measures–shareholder value analysis

Return on investment and residual income

Economic value added

Market value added

Total shareholder return

The role of the corporate centre

Regardless of the measures used, they are insufficient to fully guide managers in their decision making since they measure ends not means. There is a need to use additional measures that are not financial. Goold and Campbell looked at the styles adopted by the corporate centre and how this influenced the development of business strategy. They identified three patterns of behaviour as: strategic planning, financial control and strategic control and observed that there were differences between the approach taken in a number of strategic control situations

Regarding strategy and style

Please review the work of Goold and Campbell from the manual and, by your broader reading, try to identify examples of each style in the real world

Management accounting and performance management

Traditionally management accounting has focussed on calculating and providing management information based on resource utilisation, costs, volumes and profit. This approach has been criticised as

⇨ Not recognising the increased importance of fixed costs
⇨ Misunderstanding cost drivers
⇨ Being more concerned with cost assignment than with cost attribution

As such, they lead management to focus on unimportant processes and to misunderstand the true costs and profits from products and customers

Activity-based management (ABM)

ABM

'… the entire set of actions that can be taken, on a better informed basis, with activity-based cost information. With ABM the organisation accomplishes its outcomes with fewer demands on organisational resources; that is, the organisation can achieve the same outcomes (e.g. revenues) at a lower cost'

Management accounting and performance management

The stages in designing an ABC system are:

$\Rightarrow$ Identify major activities in the organisation
$\Rightarrow$ Create a cost pool (or cost centre) for each activity
$\Rightarrow$ Determine the cost driver for each major activity
$\Rightarrow$ Assign the costs of activities to products according to product demand for activities

Regarding activity-based management

If you are asked to recommend and devise an ABM system, make sure that you contrast it with a simple cost allocation system

Multidimensional performance measurement

It has been argued that to develop satisfactory performance measures, five 'areas of activity' are necessary:

⇨ Development of a new information architecture
⇨ Determining the necessary hardware, software and telecoms technology
⇨ Align the information system with the company's incentive system
⇨ Draw on outside resources
⇨ Design a process to ensure that the other four activities occur

Suggested development approach

⇨ Identify the key outputs required from the activity
⇨ Identify the key processes in providing the outputs
⇨ Identify the interfaces of the activity with other parts of the value network
⇨ Develop KPI's for the key processes
⇨ Identify data sources for KPIs
⇨ Develop reporting system
⇨ Review effectiveness of control system

The six-dimensional performance matrix

A model developed originally for service industries, this has six generic performance measures that are used to a greater or lesser extent in most companies. The dimensions are competitiveness, financial performance, quality of service, flexibility, resource utilisation and innovation. These dimensions can be expanded by specific performance measures appropriate to the firm in which they are being implemented

Regarding this model

Make sure that you could devise the appropriate specific measures for a service company of the examiners choice!

The balanced scorecard

A composite model of financial and non-financial measures which the authors suggest is used as a system for communication, informing, and learning not just as a control system

The system considers performance metrics under the headings of: customer perspective, financial perspective, internal business processes together with learning and growth. The following points are made:

⇨ The four perspectives are a template, not a straightjacket – others may be used, and financial measures remain important
⇨ The BSC is not the only performance measurement system that the firm should use
⇨ The BSC can be developed at the SBU or corporate level
⇨ The BSC can support both market-based and competence-based approaches to strategy
⇨ The measures used in the BSC should be mutually consistent and reinforcing

Multidimensional performance measurement

There are, however, issues with its use:

⇨ Problems in gaining management commitment
⇨ Deciding who should develop the measures
⇨ Avoiding using only the KPI's that can be measured easily
⇨ Problems of ensuring measures are congruent

Performance measurement systems

We have discussed a number of performance measurement systems in this chapter so far. You should make sure that you can compare and contrast the systems discussed and recommend the most appropriate for a particular set of circumstances. Having made the recommendation you might be asked to also recommend how the system should be implemented and the KPI's that might be used

As we have discussed earlier, stakeholder analysis has become increasingly important and it has been suggested that performance measures be developed specifically to look after their interests. Specifically these could be introduced for customers as we have seen in the models described above. However, they could also be developed to plan and monitor the relationship with suppliers. Similarly for not-for-profit organisations, measures could be developed which could be used in a modified version of the balanced scorecard

Regarding stakeholder measures

At this point you should look at the pilot paper which has a question relating to the development of a balanced scorecard for a botanical garden

Multinational industries

Control in multinational enterprises is more complex and presents a particular set of issues:

⇨ Differing economic conditions in different countries will make performance evaluation difficult

⇨ Differing legal frameworks will impose different costs on the business

⇨ Different culture and trading conditions

Transfer pricing

It is important that you revise the material you covered in *Management Accounting – Performance Measurement* on the calculation of transfer pricing. The objectives of a transfer pricing system may include:

⇨ Minimisation of import duties

⇨ Management of direct taxation

⇨ Management of indirect taxation

⇨ Repatriation of profits in kind

⇨ To win host country approval

⇨ To disguise the profitability of a subsidiary

⇨ To enable penetration pricing

There are several implications for the strategic management of multinationals. These can include:

⇨ Loss of controllability principle if country divisions are subject to central transfer prices and charges

⇨ Reduced ability to respond competitively to local market challenges

⇨ Reduced profitability compared to other MNE's

⇨ Transfer prices can affect organisational structure and ownership

⇨ The threat of imposed transfer prices conflicts with the logic of strategic management

Regarding multinationals

You should revise your material from elsewhere on the calculation of transfer prices and the behavioural impacts of the levels at which they are set. From your broader reading you might look at the types of non-financial KPI's that a multinational could incorporate into a performance system

General study tips

There can be no substitute for practice and you should look carefully at the questions that are available in both the pilot paper and the back of the manual. Additionally, where you have been referred back to an earlier manual, please practice the questions that were included there. Good Luck!